THE SIN

EUROPEAN CU

by John Redwood

The arguments for and against a single European currency
How a single European currency would be introduced
The economic consequences of the Euro
The advantages and disadvantages for business,
and the impact on democracy and on the constitution.

TOGETHER WITH:

"A global vision": a speech delivered by John Redwood to the CBI
Conference, Birmingham, November 14th 1995.

"Arguments against a single European currency"
by Hywel Williams: the contemporary and political context

"Engines of State"
by Andrew Roberts: a historical study of single currency areas and
their characteristics

TECLA
in association with the Conservative 2000 Foundation

ISBN   0-948607-23-8

Published by Tecla Editions, PO Box 7567, London NW3 2LJ. Telephone/fax 0171 435 5077.

Also available from Tecla: *John Redwood and Popular Conservatism* (ISBN 0-948607-22-X).

Printed in Great Britain by Selwood Printing, Burgess Hill, West Sussex, RH15 9UA.

First published in 1995.

CONTENTS

PREFACE

It is hard to overestimate the importance of the single European currency. It is said by some that if Britain joins it, we will enjoy ever greater prosperity; by others, that it will mean the end of any significant control of our own destiny. Whichever is true, it is clearly an issue that demands attention and debate.

This is a particularly apt moment for the publication of this book, because the single currency is being actively discussed now at the highest political levels both in Britain and in Continental Europe. The time when a decision will have to be taken about whether or not to join a single currency is coming closer and closer. Decisions are already being taken about details which would apply if we were to go ahead.

This book discusses the implications of a single European currency for British business and employment, and for democracy and the constitution, especially from the global viewpoint which John Redwood's work in the international financial world enables him to discuss from experience. Hywel Williams discusses arguments against it in the contemporary and political context. Historical precedents are set out by the distinguished historian Andrew Roberts, which cast light on what the nature of a single currency would be. A special effort has been made to express everything in approachable language while not shunning topics which are inevitably sometimes technical but which have great importance.

BRIAN JEFFERY

The Single European Currency

by The Rt. Hon. John Redwood, MP

ARGUMENTS IN FAVOUR OF A SINGLE CURRENCY

1. It is a major step on the way to a European superstate.

The main reason for wanting a single currency for the countries of Western Europe would be to create a single European government. A single currency immediately requires a single monetary authority operating Europe-wide. It means that anti-inflation policy, monetary policy, interest rate policy, foreign exchange intervention policy, budget deficits – in practice all the major economic decision making levers – have to reside at the European rather than at the member state level. Instead of urging or encouraging member states to have policies which draw ever closer together, the European institutions would be in the driving seat establishing a single European economic policy.

Once a single currency has been adopted by a group of countries the role of their Finance Ministers reduces dramatically. Norman Tebbit said the British Parliament would be rather like a rate-capped County Council. He meant by that, that European controls over the level of government borrowing and the main economic policies currently determined by or debated in the British Parliament would be settled at the European level. Parliament and British Ministers would be able to debate the distribution of the permitted level of public spending and borrowing and may have some influence on how the money was raised to pay for public services but they would lose control over most of the major items of economic policy.

A single currency is the biggest and most important step towards a European Superstate that the European institutions have proposed. A single market if it is just a free trade area does not entail any limitations of importance on the sovereignty of each member state. A single market as defined by the European Community does impose some limitations upon the freedom of action of the member states, as it includes a substantial number of proscriptive laws emanating

7

from Europe which limit the powers of member states' Parliaments to organise trade and industrial affairs in different ways. Nonetheless, the major power to control economic policies still rests with each member state.

Those who want to see a European Superstate argue it usually on general political grounds. They believe that it would prevent future wars between the European countries and would give Europe a bigger clout in the wider world. The danger could be the opposite. If countries with different histories, traditions, cultures and languages are brought together in a single state it may increase the tensions and create disagreements against the common course of action that would not have occurred if they had retained their independence. It would also mean that whereas Europe at the moment has several voices at international gatherings like the OECD and the Group of Seven, the establishment of a single European state would reduce the membership of these bodies to one and each country would only have a part share in its representation in the international body.

A single currency should be urged by all those who believe in the European Superstate as it would mean the end of national autonomy in the public policy area of overriding interest to many voters.

2. It would produce a low rate of inflation throughout Europe.

The single currency proponents believe that the new European Central Bank could and should have the virtues of the Bundesbank. Postwar Germany has followed a very successful counter-inflation policy based on a political consensus in Germany that inflation is an unmitigated evil. This strong feeling in Germany is not surprising given the terrible experiences of the Weimar inflation and the trauma of the Second World War. This political consensus was reflected in a strong independent central bank charged by the politicians through the constitution with the task of upholding the value of the currency.

The aim of currency union in Western Europe is seen by many to be similar to that of the German experience. Countries like Italy and Spain which have had poor inflation records and even a country like Britain which had a poor inflation record in the 1970s could be expected to benefit from submitting their economic policies to the control of the European Central Bank which would have as its prime aim the maintenance of price stability. The theory is that the central bank can be charged with this duty in the treaty and then given independent board members who would enforce the duty upon the member states' economies.

It is certainly true that the postwar German record on inflation has been a lot better than that of most of the other member states. The United Kingdom has shown in the last decade that it is possible to improve the inflation record of a country without a prices and income policy and usually with floating exchange rates. The Germans have shown that it is possible to follow a very successful anti-inflation strategy by means of a strong monetary policy without reference to other countries or currencies.

The European Central Bank could certainly deliver a low inflation rate across Europe under the constitution proposed. Its officials would have to do so and it would have to keep interest rates at whatever level was necessary in order to curb monetary growth. It would not do it by means of managing the exchange rate but would have to do it by internal domestic monetary policy for Europe as a whole.

The debating question is not whether it is technically possible to achieve this by means of a European Central Bank but whether there is enough agreement and consensus amongst not just the governments but also the peoples of Western Europe that this should be the prime purpose of economic policy. Do all agree that it should be delivered by independent officials without reference back to politicians and without proper Parliamentary debate concerning the other consequences? Would Europe be happy with the high real interest rates and high unemployment it might cause?

4. A single currency would get rid of transaction charges and risks for businesses and travellers handling the European currencies.

The simplest and strongest argument in favour of the single currency for Western Europe is that it would free business and individuals of currency fluctuations between marks, francs, pounds and the other European currencies and would free them of the need to pay charges and commission on switching from one currency to another. Whilst this would be bad news for bankers and for the City of London, the world's leading foreign exchange market place, it would undoubtedly save transaction costs for businesses handling a range of European currencies. It would prevent foreign exchange losses within Europe just as it would also prevent foreign exchange gain for those companies capable enough or lucky enough to manage their currency exposures to a profitable conclusion.

Some people extend this argument too far. They believe it would take all of the currency risk out of business and all of the transaction costs. Businesses in Europe typically buy their raw materials in dollars. All of the leading commodity markets including oil, the soft commodities and metals trade in dollars. Many of these European countries receive revenues not just from European countries but in a range of currencies from around the world. The advent of a single European currency for the Western European economies will still leave the companies at risk of adverse movements with the dollar relative to the ecu affecting their business. It would still leave them with all the costs involved in handling foreign currencies outside the single currency area.

It is of course quite possible for companies at the moment to avoid Foreign Exchange risk. They can do this by matching their assets and their liabilities in the same currency. They can make sure that their receivables and their costs are similarly matched and where they are not matched they can match them by forward exchange trans-actions. Whilst people argue that the present transaction costs in Foreign Exchange risk necessitate a European common currency they do not argue that the presence of similar or even greater risks and costs for the businesses trading with dollar expenses and European receivables argue in favour of us all adopting the dollar as our single currency to facilitate trade worldwide. Reluctance to argue for a single world currency – say the dollar or the yen – illustrates that the argument is about more than mere trade and transaction costs but is also about political identity and political power. Nonetheless it remains the strongest argument in favour of the single currency that for business and travellers it would simplify life to some extent.

34 A single market requires a single currency.

People who strongly believe the world is going to divide up into a select group of protected and controlled trading blocks believe that to create such a strong trading block in Europe requires the adoption of a single currency. They argue that the United States of America created a strong single market by unifying around the dollar and that it would not be possible to achieve a strong single market in Western Europe without the adoption of a single united currency.

Critics of this argument point out that the true analogy between the European Community and North America rests not between the EC and the United States of America but between the EC and the North American free trade area. The barriers to trade are being reduced between Mexico, Canada and the United States, but no-one is suggesting that the Canadian dollar and the Mexican peso have to be absorbed into the American dollar in order to get the benefits of the proper free trade area. Similarly, several Asian countries are developing a free trade area, but no-one is suggesting that they should all give up their own currencies and adopt the yen or some new trans-asian currency.

It is quite possible to get substantial benefits from a free trade area without amalgamating currencies.

ARGUMENTS AGAINST A SINGLE EUROPEAN CURRENCY

1. It is a major step on the way to a European superstate.

The main argument against a single currency is that it would be a major step on the way to a single European nation. Just as those who favour one strongly believe that the single European country and government is what we need, so those against are fundamentally opposed to the idea that the European countries can be governed as one.

Existing common policies in Europe are already creating tensions between countries. The Common Fisheries Policy, the one where the pooling of arrangements has gone furthest of all, is causing substantial tensions, especially between Spain and the rest as Spanish trawlers fish in other countries' waters and are thought to break the rules governing the amount of fish that they are allowed to catch and land. The Common Agricultural Policy produces tensions between the Southern and Northern countries over which type of products should be the principal beneficiaries and between the free traders and the protectionists more generally. The advent of a single currency with a single economic policy could increase these tensions dramatically. If one country's economic performance was poor and another one was strong within the same single currency area the poor performing economy would soon begin to object to the general economic policy, but it would have no direct means of relief as it would have ceded its right to control economic policy to the European Central Bank. The whole content of domestic policy would change dramatically. There would be little point in the United Kingdom's political parties debating general economic policy, the level of unemployment, the inflation rate, balance of payments and the other principal economic concerns either in Parliament or in General Elections. Any such debate would be empty, as whatever the parties and the people in Parliament thought the economic policy would continue to be determined by the independent officials of the European Central Bank. It is difficult to see how loyalty and harmony could be created within a multi-language country with such different histories and cultures as those represented by France, Germany, Britain, Italy and the smaller European countries.

2. Adopting a single currency would mean higher taxation.

In the United Kingdom we have a single currency area using the pound. Some parts of the single currency area are more prosperous than others. It is accepted, because we belong to a single currency area and because we have a shared history, tradition and culture, that the richer parts of the single currency area should pay higher taxes in order to make transfer payments to the poorer parts. At the moment, for example, London and the South-East accept that they should pay higher taxes in order to subsidise Liverpool and Merseyside. There have of course been times in our history when Merseyside was a very successful part of the United Kingdom economically and was itself carrying some of the burden of cross-subsidisation to poorer parts. Whilst there are arguments about the effectiveness of some of these transfer payments, no-one challenges the principle that underlies them. The richer and stronger parts of the single currency area have duties and obligations towards the poorer and weaker parts.

If we created a single currency area in Western Europe these obligations would have to be recognised to extend much more widely than merely from London to Liverpool. London and the South-East of England would be a relatively rich part of the wider European single currency area, especially if it included Southern Italy, Portugal,

12

Spain, Greece, Ireland, Eastern Germany and the more deprived parts of France beyond the Parisian metropolitan area. Taxpayers in London and the South-East would have to accept that they should pay higher bills in order to cross-subsidise these weaker and poorer parts of the European currency area.

It is by no means clear that European sentiment has built up to the point in the United Kingdom where people would want to pay higher taxes in order to cross-subsidise what are at the moment other countries. Nor is it by any means clear that the United Kingdom economy as a whole would benefit from the higher taxation that this would necessitate. At the moment membership of the European community costs the British taxpayer ten thousand million pounds a year in extra taxation or four pence on the standard rate of income tax. Some two-thirds of this money is returned in the form of public expenditure payments in the United Kingdom especially in the form of payments to farmers. A single currency area would both increase the total amount of taxation that would have to be raised and would increase the amount spent outside the United Kingdom as a whole.

Taxes are already high. They are making their impact on family budgets and on enterprise. Preventing us reducing taxes or requiring us to increase them as the single currency scheme would do could well do economic damage to a country which requires lower taxes to increase its prosperity.

3. A single currency would lead to higher prices.

The European commission has stated that in the transition period, it is quite likely that manufacturers and shopkeepers would take advantage of the need to reprice everything in a new currency to put their prices up. The evidence of decimalization confirms that this is very likely to happen. When British coinage was decimalized we moved from a penny which was one two hundred and fortieth of a pound to a penny which was one hundredth of a pound. This substantially reduced the sensitivity of the coinage at pricing lower priced items. Moving from the pound to the ecu would be very confusing to many people. It would be like going shopping in a foreign currency in the early months after the transition, with many people losing their sense of values in the new currency.

You could not blame companies for taking advantage of the introduction of a new currency to increase prices and to raise margins somewhat. It would of course be easier for this to occur in markets where there is a monopoly or monopoly elements. There are those who argue for a single currency who wish to pursue a protectionist policy towards European business. If these two policies were introduced together then it would undoubtedly produce higher prices at the expense of real incomes and the amounts that people could consume. The European Central Bank would strive to prevent there being an overall inflation. The increase of prices would simply transfer well-being from consumers to producers who would then spend it on their own inefficiencies as the protectionist policies would inevitably lead to a less efficient European industry.

4. The high cost of transition.

In order to introduce a single currency a huge number of computer programmes and machines would have to be changed. Every cash dispenser, every till, every slot machine, each car parking ticket machine, drinks machine and turnstile would need changing. Every business accounting programme, bank telling machine and payroll programme would need changing. The sheer physical task of withdrawing all the coins currently in circulation in the European community countries and minting an entirely new set sufficient for three hundred and fifty million people would be a very expensive and time consuming task.

Businesses which are entirely domestic would have all the costs and none of the benefits. There would be no advantage for them in the reduced transaction costs in foreign currencies, whilst they would have to renew all of their equipment if it collected or calculated monetary amounts. Even those which did have transaction costs in foreign currencies that it could reduce or save as a result of the single currency would have transitional and equipment costs far outstripping the likely benefits for many years to come.

The main beneficiaries would be the business machine manufacturers. They would have a bonanza in re-equipping British industry with ecu equipment to replace sterling. It would also be very good news for private sector banks, note printers and for the public sector mint producing the coins. The costs have been estimated at well over a billion pounds for the United Kingdom alone to carry out all the necessary work.

5. Preparing for the single currency would cause considerable economic disruption.

The original scheme for the single currency included spending two years in the narrow band of the exchange rate mechanism ensuring that currencies are behaving similarly to each other before irrevocably locking the currencies together as the final preparation for issuing the single currency. In the amended version of the scheme, not in the Treaty, currencies would be locked without necessarily having performed together in the bands of the exchange rate mechanism which have anyway been substantially widened as the result of the pressures in the exchange rate mechanism in recent years.

The United Kingdom's experience in the exchange rate mechanism was far from encouraging. In the late 1980s the United Kingdom was de facto in the exchange rate mechanism by shadowing the Deutschmark as preparation for entering the mechanism. During this period the pound wished to rise out of the bands identified for it. The government took action to try to prevent the pound rising. Firstly, it kept interest rates lower than was desirable for domestic monetary reasons. As a result people borrowed much more and the money supply expanded more rapidly. Secondly, a large number of pounds were printed and sold in the foreign exchange markets to try to keep the pound down. A lot of this money passed into the banking system. It was used to advance more loans, expanding the money supply further and generating inflation.

By the time the United Kingdom did enter the Exchange Rate Mechanism inflation was already well set and the pound soon came under pressure in a downwards direction. As a result the United Kingdom had to set interest rates much higher for much longer than was desirable for domestic monetary purposes and the reverse process occurred over the foreign exchanges. The government had to buy in a large number of pounds, depleting its foreign exchange reserves. It needed to borrow substantial sums of money in foreign currencies in order to play the exchanges. This process reinforced the recessionary forces created by the very high interest rates which the exchange rate mechanism necessitated. The more pounds that the government brought in, the less money was in circulation within the banking system for on lending to industry and commerce. As a result Britain's period in the Exchange Rate Mechanism was characterised by the onset of an extremely sharp recession, a large number of business failures and a rapid increase in unemployment.

The United Kingdom has not been alone in its experiences with the Exchange Rate Mechanism. Whilst advocates of the ERM have always said that if we followed sensible disciplines all would be well and that it was a necessary discipline to control inflation, other countries had similar problems in trying to peg their currency to the Deutschmark. The French in recent years have been most successful, creating a strong franc closely aligned to the Deutschmark. The price of their success has been a very high and rising level of unemployment and higher interest rates than would be necessary for domestic economic purposes. Other countries have been far less successful than France in keeping their currencies in line with the Deutschmark although they too have experienced higher and rising unemployment as a result of the high interest rates that they have used to attempt to hold their currencies in line. The Italians, the Spaniards and some of the smaller countries have all been through devaluations despite Exchange Rate Mechanism discipline. Preparation for a single currency will increase the tension that they have seen in the system in the past.

With the possible exception of the Benelux countries and Germany the economies of Western Europe are not in line with one another and they are not sufficiently interdependent to make so called convergence of their performance easy to achieve. Re- entry into the Exchange Rate Mechanism or entry into tight narrow bands for existing members would cause exactly the same stresses that we have seen in the past. There is no single perfect rate which you can select which would then mean perpetual harmony and discipline within the system. Your entry rate may at the beginning be too low but as the economies' performances differ it may become too high sometime later or vice versa. What is clear is that ERM experience has been characterised by a movement to much higher unemployment across Western Europe. In part this can be laid at the door of the Exchange Rate Mechanism which has meant higher interest rates in Western Europe than otherwise would have been chosen and higher than many of the more competitive parts of the world. In part it can be attributed to labour market inflexibility which has also characterised Western European policy on the continent in recent years.

At least the Exchange Rate Mechanism gave a warning and provided a clear indication as to whether economies were in line sufficiently for them to be able to join a single currency or whether a further period of convergence was required. The idea that the currencies for the single union could move to a locked position and stay there whilst necessary preparation work was completed for convergence to the single currency is an especially dangerous one. The irrevocable locking of currencies means that none of the normal adjustment processes can take place. If there is still a free market in the currencies as we presume there would be, the currency speculators could easily take on the Central Banks in the system and it could rapidly become unsustainable. It definitely means that the different countries within the system will have their economies put under pressure by being expected to perform to a common standard with common interest rates and common policies long before there is any evidence that they are equipped to do so. If free trade in currencies is abandoned it is difficult to see how normal settlements and transactions can be accomplished.

6. A single market could be damaged by a single currency.

There is a long way to go in Western Europe before there is a truly open free market amongst the member states. It would have been possible to have created a free market by the single legal rule, that if a product or service is of merchandisable quality in one state then it can be sold in another state. It would then have been up to the customers in that other country to decide whether they agreed with the regulators of the exporting state or not. If they agreed they would have been able to buy the product whatever their own regulators thought and if they disagreed the exporting state and its companies would have to modify its standards and regulations if it wished to achieve foreign sales. In place of this simple idea which was reflected in the Cassis De Dijon judgement, the European Community decided to proceed by passing a large volume of harmonising and regulatory legislation. Whilst this legislation is in some areas opening markets and encouraging more trade, in other areas it merely became a new brake on business performance and a new restriction on innovation. A large number of product Directives have the purpose of creating minimum standards and imposing quality requirements on any producer. They can also have the consequence of making experimentation or innovation illegal to produce a better standard or specification. In areas like aviation and telecommunications where there was a great need to deregulate to allow proper market access community wide for successful companies, there has been some stumbling or hesitation about going the whole way and deregulating.

Instead of wishing to get on with proper market opening along these lines, many advocates of community progress have said that the next main impediment to single market development that needs removal is the existence of competing currencies. It is difficult to see why creating a monopoly in an area in place of competition could ever be good news for trade. There is nothing stopping the businesses and people of Western Europe at the moment electing to do their business in ecus if that is the best way of doing it. The United Kingdom government has been particularly active in trying to encourage an ecu market by issuing ecu instruments of its own and encouraging others to borrow or lend in ecus. The fact is that the businesses or people of Western Europe do not find the ecu a particularly useful or helpful currency in which to deal or transact business.

Far from becoming the motor of economic growth, the ecu scheme could become, like the regulatory single market scheme, an impediment to business opportunity and development. The single market measures finally came into full effect at the beginning of 1993. The Cecchini Report had said that the single market would provide a boost of some 3% to European growth when it came into effect. It is therefore surprising that in the two years of the final introduction and completion of the single market in the United Kingdom, the years in which the largest numbers of new measures came into effect when they had their chance to prove their worth, the economy actually contracted rather than increased. It is difficult to believe that the recession in the United Kingdom would have been 3% deeper had it not been for the single market. Indeed the import and export figures seem to contradict this idea. The single market was overhyped in the Cecchini Report and the failure to deliver a genuinely open market in crucial fast growing areas like telecommunications and financial services means that the results have been extremely disappointing. To lock the European currencies into a fixed rate for several years in preparation for a single currency would be likely to provide a further brake to Western European growth.

Countries would no longer be able to find through market forces that level of currency which encouraged freer trade and more competitiveness on their part. They would be saddled with levels of interest rates and borrowing controls that could do damage to growth prospects. As a result it is very likely that the single currency scheme for those embarking on it would see higher unemployment and less economic opportunity than if we continued with competing currencies where people and businesses can make their own choices about which one to use.

7. A single European currency would do considerable damage to democracy.

The House of Commons would be a strange place without any debates on the progress of the economy, economic growth, unemployment, inflation, mortgage rates and interest rates generally. Yet that is in effect what we are invited to accept if we agree to the single currency, the independent central bank and the main economic policies being determined by our elected officials at that central bank. Coupled with strong continental demands for a common social policy through the social chapter which Tony Blair would like to adopt in the United Kingdom and the wish to see much more co-operative activity in the defence and foreign affairs fields, we would be well on the way to Westminster having little function. There would then, indeed, be a democratic deficit.

At the moment there need not be any democratic deficit. The Council of Ministers is the legislature. Member states each send a Minister or representative to the legislature. It is quite possible for Members of Parliament to debate fully and exhaustively any draft proposals that are coming before the Council of Ministers in good time before the decision-making meeting. A sensible democracy organises itself to accommodate draft proposals that are sent out to domestic Parliamentarians. Debates are held before the ministerial meeting and if necessary a scrutiny reserve is placed on the agreement around the table saying that the country will only confirm its agreement to this proposal if Parliament is in accord with the proposal as amended by the Council of Ministers. This system can work if the volume of legislation is kept within reasonable bounds and if the legislation confines itself to that limited number of things which can best be done in co-operation with other member states. The system would break down if practically all important legislation were handled by the European Community and if other crucial decisions about the economy were taken by Community institutions.

The main democratic deficit which the single currency would create would be the inability of national or European Parliamentarians to have any decisive influence or control over the workings of the central bank and the common economic policy. It is difficult to see how this could be sustained. An economic policy on auto-pilot is a novelty which we have not seen in operation in democratic countries before.

There would be ways of attacking the democratic deficit and reducing the single currency's impact. It could be accepted that it is a major step on the road to a European super-state and powers could be given to the European Parliament to form a common economic policy and to be the controlling body to whom the European Central Bank reports. Alternatively, it would be possible for national Parliaments to provide some control over their national representatives on the central bank body if that body were reconstituted into having national representatives instead of independent people charged with implementing the treaty. Neither of these models is particularly satisfactory. It is difficult to see how the European Parliament would provide good strong control over this body when we still do not fight European elections with single European parties with clear manifestos and a clear relationship to their domestic electorates. The Parliament is too remote from the electorate to carry clout or to maintain trust. Nor would it be particularly satisfactory for there to be strong domestic control over the national representative, only to see the bank thwarted by endless bickering or your own national representative consistently outvoted on the issues that matter to you.

It has to be accepted that the single currency model is part of a view of the world which believes that big centralised government is better than devolved smaller government and believes that an elite should make the decisions for us without any particular democratic accountability. It is difficult to believe that the British people would like such a system.

8. It would mean transferrring our foreign exchange reserves to the European Bank.

The United Kingdom has twenty-five thousand million pounds of foreign exchange reserves. It is in effect the nation's savings bank account providing the money to intervene in foreign exchange markets and to provide for future liabilities. Under a single currency scheme this money would have to transfer to the control of the European Central Bank. It effectively means pooling the savings of European countries in a common system. From the national point of view it would be sensible to repay as much government borrowing as possible out of the foreign exchange reserves prior to transfer to minimise the amount of money we have to surrender. If every member state acted in its own interest in this way then the foreign exchange reserves of the new system would be quite modest in scale. A central bank may object to this or it may see it as a sensible constraint upon its aim of intervening in dollar and yen markets on behalf of the ecu.

Such a proposal would only work if people really did feel their allegiance was to a country called Europe rather than a country called the United Kingdom. Otherwise it is difficult to see what we get back in return for surrendering our twenty-five thousand million pounds of hard earned savings. We would have the continuing pleasure of paying the interest bill on the borrowings and the new European Central Bank would have the pleasure of using the money as they saw fit.

9. Joining a single currency means European Community control over government spending, taxation and borrowing levels.

Under the rules of the single currency scheme it has been agreed that there should be controls on the level of the budget deficit. This is a necessary precaution in a single currency area as countries will be borrowing at a common interest rate which will not reflect their underlying credit risk or degree of past borrowing unless they reach the point where people think they would renege on their pledges. It is clearly in the interests of any individual member country of the currency union to place controls on the borrowing levels of the other countries. If no such controls were placed then several member states could decide to expand their budget deficits to take advantage of the general level of interest rates. In applying the process they would lumber the other member states with a higher interest rate than would otherwise be the case because of the volume of borrowing by those member states.

It is a small step from saying that the European Community has the right, indeed the duty, to control the level of deficit to saying that it would also take an interest in the level of spending and taxation. This has not yet appeared on the European agenda but it is difficult to believe that within a single currency area it would be long coming. It would be quite possible to argue in such a situation that in the interest of convergence and fair play similar levels of public spending and taxation should apply throughout the economic area. If the United Kingdom persisted in having lower tax and spending than other countries, so the argument would run, the United Kingdom would gain an economic advantage from this which would be unfair. The convergence criteria would also include a proportion of the existing stock of debt. This again is a important precaution, as any country coming into the single currency area with a well above average stock of debt relative to its gross domestic product will be a winner at the expense of the others because it would be able to renew its debt at the lower general interest rate that would apply whilst at the same time increasing the interest rate of those countries that have a more modest stock of debt.

Because the United Kingdom is at the low end of the scale both in terms of its current running deficit and particularly in terms of the stock of debt which it would carry into a single currency area it would be net loser on both counts. It would tend to have to pay higher interest rates than would otherwise be the case because of the higher past and present borrowing levels of the other members of the union.

The union is also likely to get interested not only in the level of deficits or the general level of taxation but also the specific incidence of taxation. We have already seen proposals for individual community taxes in areas like copyright protection. We already have one harmonised tax which we all had to impose in the form of value added tax. A single currency area would be likely to produce more common taxes both to raise the revenue base to pay for the common government and as instruments of policy as an expression of the power of that European government.

HOW A SINGLE CURRENCY WOULD BE INTRODUCED BY THE EUROPEAN COMMUNITY

Under the Treaty of Rome as amended by Maastricht, clear guidance is laid out on how a single currency could be created and how a common economic policy will be developed.

Under Article 103, the Council is charged by qualified majority with drawing up an economic policy for the member states and the community. The Council is charged with the duty of monitoring economic developments in each of the member states on the advice of the Commission, making sure that the economic policies of each country are in line with the guidelines that they have set up. If a member state steps out of line, the Council can make recommendations to that state to change its policy. Under Article 104, member states are told to avoid excessive government deficits. Under the protocol an excessive deficit is defined as 3% of gross domestic product at market prices and the ratio of government debt to gross domestic product at 60%. The deficit definition includes central government, regional and local government and social security funds.

Where the Council decides there is an excessive deficit it produces recommendations to the member state to bring that situation to an end within a given period. If there is no effective action taken in response to the recommendations, the Council can make its recommendations public. If the member state still persists in failing to put into practice the recommendations of the Council, Council can repeat its instructions and demand reports to monitor progress. If the member states still persists in its failure to take the necessary action the European Investment Bank might be invited to reconsider its lending policy. The member state might be asked to make a non-interest bearing deposit with the Community until the day the excessive deficit has been corrected. In the final resort fines can be imposed.

There are such strict rules on excessive deficits because a currency union requires control by all the constituent parts over the amount of borrowing at the common interest rate.

Article 105 of the treaty describes the objectives of the European system of central banks. The prime objective is that of price stability. The European system of central banks has to define and implement the monetary policy of the Community, conduct foreign exchange operations, hold and manage the official foreign reserves and promote the smooth operations of the payment system. The European system of central banks is controlled by the European Central Bank itself.

Article 105 (a) gives the European Central Bank the exclusive right to authorise the issue of bank notes within the community. Member states are given the right to issue coins subject to approval by the European Central Bank, which controls the volume of the issue. The Council can act to ensure harmonised denominations and technical specifications of all the coins intended for circulation.

Article 106 describes the European System of Central Banks which will be governed by the European Central Bank and its governing council and executive board. Article 107 seeks to guarantee the independence not only of the European Central Bank but also of the central banks of each member state. It bans any member of their decision making bodies from seeking or taking instructions from any government of a member state, from any community institution or any other body. The idea is that the governors of the European Central Bank and of the member state national banks should be without outside influence or control, dedicated to the principles of the treaty and especially to the creation of price stability. Article 108 instructs each member state to bring its legislation for its own central bank into line with these requirements. Article 108 (a) gives the European Central Bank the power to make legislation which will be binding on all member states and have general application. Under Article 109, the council is given the power to settle foreign exchange intervention policy although it has to be consistent with the primary objective of the European Central Bank to maintain and create price stability. Under this article the Council is given power to take the ecu and the Community into an ERM type system with currencies that are outside the single currency.

Article 109 sets out the institutional provisions for the European Central Bank. The Executive Board includes the President, the Vice President and four other members. They have to be appointed from among persons of recognised standing and professional experience in monetary or banking matters by common agreement of the governments of the member states. They will be given a term of office of eight years which will not be renewable. They have to be nationals of member states.

The treaty then turns to discussing the transitional period before the introduction of the single currency. A monetary committee with advisory status is to be set up to keep under review the monetary and financial policies of the member states and report to the Council and Commission. At the start of the third stage of Monetary Union, an Economic and Financial Committee will replace the Monetary Committee. This Economic and Financial Committee will provide opinions to the Council or Commission, review the economic and financial situation of the member states and examine at least once a year the situation concerning the movement of capital and the freedom of payments. The member states, the Commission and the European Central Bank should each appoint two members of the committee. The second stage for achieving economic and monitory union began on the first of January 1994, under Article 109(e). Each member state was required to have freed capital movements and to adopt policies likely to produce the economic convergence necessary to equip them for economic and monetary union. They are also required to begin creating a truly independent central bank. The European Monetary Institute was established, managed by a council consisting of a president and the governors of the national central banks. The aim of this Monetary Institute is to strengthen co-operation between national central banks, strengthen co-ordination of monetary policies, monitor the functioning of the European Monetary System, take over the task of the Euro Monetary Co-operation Fund and facilitate the use of the ecu. Article 109(h) acknowledges that with this system based on keeping currencies in line with one another, member states might get into difficulties with their balance of payments. The response under the treaty is to allow protectionist measures to be taken if the deficit proves persistent. This power only lasts until the third stage of the Monetary Union commences.

Article 109(j) sets out the most important convergence criteria that member states are expected to meet prior to going on to Monetary Union. They are required to achieve a high degree of price stability. In the protocol this is defined as a rate that does not exceed by more than one and a half percentage points that of the three best performing member states in terms of low inflation rates. Secondly, they should avoid excessive deficits defined as avoiding violation of the excessive deficits requirement of less than 3% of GDP for the running deficit and less than 60% of GDP for the stock of debt. Thirdly, each member state should have observed the normal fluctuation margins provided by the ERM for at least two years without devaluing against the currency of any member state. Fourthly, long term interest rates should not exceed by more than two percentage points those of the best three performing member states in terms of price stability. By the 31st of December 1996, the Council should decide whether a majority of the member states fulfil these conditions necessary for the adoption of a single currency and decide whether it is sensible for the Community to enter the third stage. If by the end of 1997 the date of the beginning of the third stage has not been set the third stage will automatically start on the 1st of January 1999. In practice much of this has been overtaken by events. It has now been accepted by the Community that the third stage will start on the 1st of January 1999 and not earlier. The exchange rate mechanism has been torn apart by market pressures. The old system of narrow and wide ERM bands has been scrapped and replaced by a very wide band of 15%. In its place the idea is that between 1999 and 2003, there will be four years of fixed exchange rates for those currencies that are going to join the single currency system.

Once the decision has been taken to go to the third stage, the European Central Bank is established and takes over from the EMI. At the beginning of the third stage, the Council acting on the basis of unanimity of all those member states entering the single currency decides the conversion rates to which the currencies will be irrevocably fixed and converted into the ecu.

Much of the detail of the treaty is in the Protocols attached to it. The protocol on the Euro System of Central Banks is particularly strong in finding ways of limiting the authority of the member states over Central Banks and ensuring that it complies with the general will. It also gives a central bank governor additional grounds for comfort over his tenure, giving him a right to take a case to the Court of Justice if he feels his dismissal in any way infringes the Treaty requirements designed to protect his independence. He is also given a minimum term of five years under the protocol. Under Article 19 of the protocol on the European Central Banking system the European Central Bank is given the power to require credit

26

institutions in member states to hold minimum reserves on account with the ECP and National Central Banks. This means that banking regulation currently conducted by the United Kingdom Government and the Bank of England would pass into European hands and would enable the European Central Bank to have a decisive influence on whether or not London remained as a premier banking centre. The starting capital of the European Central Bank is laid down as five thousand million ecu or around four thousand million pounds. The European Central Bank would also be provided by the National Central Banks with foreign reserve assets of fifty thousand million ecu or around forty thousand million pounds. Each member state and its Central Bank is required to make a subscription as a percentage of the total. The percentage is calculated on the basis of 50% of the share of each member state in the population in the Community and 50% of the share of the member state in the gross domestic product of the Community. Articles 48 and 49 allow levies for the capital foreign reserves of the central bank to be in place even on those countries not joining the single currency system if the Council decides that is necessary to pay the bills. The United Kingdom does not have an exemption from this particular clause of the protocol.

The United Kingdom's position is different from all other countries, although Denmark too is not bound to stage 3 under a separate protocol. The United Kingdom retains the right to decide whether it wishes to join the third stage or not. If it decides not, it specifically retains its powers in the field of monetary policy according to national law. It is also exempted from some of the requirements relating to the European system of Central Banks and of course would make no contribution to choosing the people running the European Central Bank itself.

The complicated three-phase structure demonstrates the great difficulty of getting different countries in Western Europe into a monetary union in the first place. The second stage is designed to be difficult. The convergence criteria, whilst thought by many member states to be tough, are the bare minimum required to give any chance of success to a single currency following their implementation. If member states' rates of inflation, interest rates and deficits are not in line with each other the stresses and strains of the single currency area would be unacceptably large. Unfortunately for those who wish to see a Single European Currency, events have been very unkind to the scheme already. Europe is further away than ever from having a set of currency rates that are stable and aligned one with another. There are very few countries anywhere near meeting the deficit requirements, as most European countries have borrowed too much already and are still running up very large deficits year by year. Even though the inflation and interest rate requirements are relative and not absolute requirements some member states are still a long way away from reaching the levels laid down in the protocol.

In 1998 when the community has to make a decision about moving to the third stage from 1999 onwards it will have a tough task. Sensible people will say that the scheme should be abandoned. If countries can't keep their currencies within 15% of each other for more than a few months at a time they are certainly not ready to lock their currency rates irrevocably and then to move to a single currency. If countries can't get their Government deficits below 5 or 6% of GDP they are simply ill-equipped for dealing with the rigorous system designed under the treaty. Of course the Community might decide that the political objective of creating a single country with a single currency is so overriding that the stresses and strains of the transitional period are less important. In this case the Community could decide to change or abandon the criteria so that more countries could qualify. Governments should be warned by markets. The markets showed what they thought of the European single currency ideal when the ERM was burst asunder and most currencies had to leave their parity with the Deutschmark. The stresses and strains would be much greater if Europe seriously went about locking its currencies together irrevocably in 1999. There would then only be two ways forward. One would be to abandon the whole scheme in the face of relentless pressure on the foreign exchanges. The other would be to cancel national currencies immediately and lock economies irrevocably into each other by issuing a single currency on the spot. The stresses and strains that are visible in the currency markets would then be visible in the dole queues and the poor economic performance of many western European countries. If a country cannot adjust its currency it will always take time to adjust its competitiveness. The result will be much higher unemployment.

A Single Currency?

The President of the CBI at their 1995 Annual Conference called for a public debate on the single currency. He asked for a rational discussion of the benefits and disadvantages for business. I agree with him that the country needs just such a public dialogue, in good time before the government is asked by our partners to amend or modify the Maastricht Treaty or to accelerate what will otherwise be a very slow road to monetary union for just a few continental countries.

What was less impressive about the CBI call was their choice of speakers for their own debate. From the platform the CBI heard from those like Sir Leon Brittan who strongly support economic and monetary union, and from those who think we should wait and see and in the meantime do not discuss the pros and cons of the issue. It was left to another business organisation to give a platform to those of us who think European policy needs changing, to put the interests of the peoples of Europe first.

I can understand and respect those who want to live in a country called Europe rather than in a country called France or Germany or Britain. I can understand their view that adopting a single currency would be a mighty step on the road to creating such a state. I am strongly opposed for a whole variety of reasons. I only ask that this, the biggest issue of our times and one of the biggest issues ever to confront our nation, should be properly debated. It is something which the people themselves must decide, after politicians, business leaders and opinion formers have staged a full debate to illuminate the subject. What worries me, as a democrat, is the way so many seem to want to sweep the issues under the carpet, to claim that a common monetary or social policy is a technical matter which has no real bearing on who we are, where we belong, or how we are governed.

I cannot see how the question of abolishing the pound is one for company treasurers or economists alone. Abolish the pound, and the power to decide interest rates, what to do with your foreign exchange reserves, how much the country can borrow and how fast money and the economy will grow passes from British institutions to European ones. The powers pass from British democratic control into the hands of unelected officials. Some will argue that this is a good idea: that we would be better off in a new country called Europe, that they might manage it better. Many will agree with me that this would be very damaging to us. But surely all can agree that for better or worse this is a massive transfer of power and responsibility, that our constitution would have changed in a fundamental way if we signed up for the ecu.

The government's position is to wait and see. I agree with John Major when he says that a single currency is extremely unlikely. I would go further, and say that under Maastricht it is impossible. To proceed the member states will need to amend or modify the Treaty. That is what the governments of France and Germany will wish to do. We must be ready with the arguments, as they would need our consent to change the Treaty, and we should have a view if they try to proceed by sidestepping it.

We should be ready for the debates about how to rescue monetary union. We should remind the Germans that we and they rightly thought when the Treaty was drafted that the conditions for convergence should be strict. We both agreed that if a country could not keep its currency in line with the DM, then its economy was not ready for monetary union. It would be dangerous to change that opinion now. We should explain to the French that merging their currency with Germany would remove freedom of French action in economic policy. It would be a strange move for M. Chirac to make, when his other policies are reasserting the independence of France whatever the international reaction. A currency union between Germany and France would be at the expense of jobs in France, and would be extremely difficult for France to break out of at a later date when the full economic costs became apparent.

The British government has also said that the U.K. will not enter the union unless it is in the British national interest to do so. I think we should debate how it could ever be in the British national interest to merge our economy with Germany and pass our powers over it to an international body. Can it really be in our national interest to go a long way towards abolishing the nation's power of self-government? What possible benefits could there be from abolishing the pound?

Business sometimes suggests that a single market needs a single currency to work well. They point to the common market of North America and say that it works better because the USA is a large area using one currency, the dollar. They ignore the fact that Mexico and Canada, also part of NAFTA, keep their own currencies.

It is clearly true that business would save the costs of exchanging one currency for another if we moved over to the ecu. It is true that business would take no more exchange risk between the DM, pound and franc. Business sees this as bringing a welcome stability after years of currency fluctuations.

Patrick Minford at Liverpool University has recently calculated what impact fixed exchange rates and a single currency have on prices and output. His findings, set out at the CBI Conference in November 1995, are fascinating. He has discovered that a single currency doubles the scale of the changes in output and prices compared with floating exchange rates, and fixed exchange rates double the variability again. In other words, a single currency would be destabilising for business and a fixed exchange rate system like the ERM doubly destabilising. Whilst exchange rate changes are a concern to some businesses, big changes in prices and output are an even bigger worry to all businesses. The stability of exchange rates would be bought at an unacceptably high price of instability in other areas that matter more to more businesses.

A large number of businesses in Britain are small and serve only a local or national market. They would, by definition, receive no benefit at all from a single currency, yet they would incur large costs. They would suffer the greater variability of output and prices which would make business planning so much more difficult. They would have to change or re-programme all their business equipment to handle ecus rather than pounds. They would suffer from the deflationary policies which would precede entering the single currency as we tried to hold the pound in line with the DM.

This is not all abstruse theory or speculation. It is not just my view, or the view of Professor Minford. It is everyone's direct experience, as we had a trial run during our period as members of the Exchange Rate Mechanism. Business was enthusiastic about going in. Those of us who had worries were told that we were wrong or prejudiced: that we did not understand businesses' needs for stability.

I found this argument most worrying. In 1989*, before we entered the ERM, I set out why I thought ERM membership would not work and would damage British business. I wrote (in 'Europe, the Good and the Bad', Centre for Policy Studies, 1989):

"Whether Britain should join the EMS or not is coming to be taken as a litmus test of being pro or anti Europe. This is absurd.

"The idea behind the European monetary system is that all currencies should be fixed at fairly stable rates between each other; and that these rates should be maintained through ever vigilant central banks intervening across the exchanges. As a result, exporters and importers should see their risks reduced as they can with some confidence predict the exchange rates from year to another. Even better, convergence of interest rates and inflation rates should result from a knowledge that currencies are going to be stable one against the other.

"The idea of the EMS is theoretically flawed. The history of the pound against the DM over the last year illustrates why this is so. Despite government efforts to get the pound to shadow the DM and to hold it around the level of 3DM to the pound, there have been periods of intense pressure leading to substantial fluctuations around that level.

"The main method for trying to keep the currencies in line is the sale or purchase of quantities of the given currency by the European central banks acting in concert or individually.

"This action is intrinsically destabilising. If the Bank of England sells a large amount of sterling in order to buy DMs, it then has a monetary problem. If it simply creates the pounds it has sold, it adds directly to the money supply. Foreign banks and other buyers then have more pounds at their disposal... This produces upward pressure on the British price level, causing inflationary worries and forcing a further rise in interest rates.

"The Bank does have some means of trying to offset this monetary problem. It put itself into the ridiculous position of selling large quantities of gilt edged securities to the private sector in order to counteract the monetary expansion caused by the intervention. In the year to March 1988 a government which collected £3.6 billion more in taxes than it spent on public goods and services had nonetheless to borrow an additional £7000 million through the gilt edged market in order to counterbalance the short term monetary consequences of trying to shadow the DM. This has burdened British taxpayers for 20 to 25 years with an additional £700 million a year of interest charges.

"If the British authorities had not been trying to shadow the DM, monetary interest rate and even exchange rate policy might have been more stable."

That seemed obvious at the time. We triggered an inflation by trying to keep the pound down to only 3DM when it wanted to go up. We then formally joined the ERM and intensified the recession by trying to keep the pound up close to 3DM when it wanted to go down. When we needed to curb monetary growth in a boom the system made us cut interest rates and stoke up inflation. When we needed to relax money growth to cure a recession the system made us keep rates too high.

Few businessmen looking back on the ERM experience would now say that it helped their businesses. Some have now changed their minds, and agree that on reflection it did not work out as they had hoped. It showed them that controlling the value of the pound for a bit, and removing that uncertainty, caused far greater instability in everything else, in the real issues of output and costs, that made life a lot more difficult for them.

Some do not wish to admit that it was a wrong idea. They say that what went wrong was the rate we entered at. If only we had gone in at 2.5 DM (or maybe, looking at today's rate, at 2.20 or 2.30) all would have been well. At the time there was agreement that it was the right time - and therefore the right rate - to go in at. At the time the pound wanted to go up, and so there were fears that the rate was too low. The truth is that there is no right rate to go in at. The German economy and the British one are different, on different economic and electoral cycles. There is no single rate of exchange that will remain right. Whichever one you choose to go into the ERM, sooner or later the strains will show and you will be forced into taking wrong policy decisions for the British commercial and industrial interest.

Some will say this is just a history lesson of no great relevance to a single currency. I said myself in 1989:

"It is difficult to see how belonging to the EMS makes this (the creation of a single currency) any more likely. The EMS depends upon the concerted action of 12 independent central banks. The creation of a single European currency would require a single European central bank combined with a single central European currency issuing authority and mint. This in turn would require a pan-European government in order to provide some political control over the actions of that central bank. Interest rate, currency and monetary policy lie at the core of government authority."

Instead of tackling the issues of a single European government head on, some have tried to sidle up to it through the question of money. Whilst I still think it impossible to peg the European currencies together successfully for any length of time, I do see now the connection in the official European mind between the ERM and a single currency. It was designed as a staging post. It then became a necessary condition, to show that economies were converging and could live happily together as one economy. It was certainly a wise safeguard to put into the Maastricht Treaty, for if currencies cannot live together in peace and stability they are not ready for marriage.

Some now say, ignoring the Treaty, that Europe must rush onto currency union regardless of the ERM. To do so would intensify the instability of the system rather than remove it. Take the exchange rate away, and all of the strains and tensions will be taken in the real economy. Instead of the franc going down a little against the DM, factories would close in France and people lose their jobs. That is not a good way to woo the people of Europe to a single government.

British business would lose out from a single currency. The City of London would not merely lose foreign exchange dealing, where it has the number one position in the world. It would come under a new type of banking regulation from Frankfurt which could drive foreign banks out of London. London has succeeded as a world marketplace using Anglo-Saxon law codes and regulations. The continental system which would underlie a new European structure has not proved nearly so successful in winning business.

British exporters who have been enjoying a heyday since we came out of the ERM, would no longer have a favourable exchange rate to help them. In current conditions a European currency would be heavily influenced by the DM. German exporters today are finding life extremely difficult with the value of their currency, and a great deal of investment and production is being shifted offshore to cope with the high level of the currency.

Business should think long and hard before signing up to the extra instability of output and prices that the ecu would mean. Many were wrong about the ERM. To have a single currency under the Treaty we would have to spend two years in the ERM again to qualify. I

34

do not hear many business volunteers for that. Why then doesn't the CBI say simply 'No' to a single currency, as it cannot be to their benefit? It is interesting to see the waning support in the business community, and the growing number of successful businesses and businessmen prepared to say they do not want one.

For the nation as a whole there are not just economic issues at stake. There are huge constitutional issues. Do we wish to remain a nation or not? We are united with one monarch, one Parliament, one army and one currency. Take away the pound, and with it many of the powers of Parliament, and you are dissolving the nation. In a world of a single currency there would be no point in writing to your MP to complain of unemployment, inflation, house prices or mortgage rates. All these things would be determined or influenced by the Central Bank, not by ourselves. There would be no point in the CBI including in its budget submission views on interest rates or the general state of trade. These matters would all be on autopilot at the Central Bank.

I believe it is a small minority of the British people who want to wind up Britain and create a new European nation with a single European government. Similarly it is a small minority who want us to turn our backs on the Common Market and deny we have interests in Europe. The British government should speak up for our idea of co-operating nation states, who preserve the right to independent action in the crucial areas of policy. It is an idea that dominates in Britain and is much more popular with people on the continent than their politicians would like us to believe. If we give voice to it with verve and distinction we could save Europe from the economic and constitutional turmoil that a single currency would cause.

Business was foolish not to listen to rational concerns about the ERM. It would be a tragedy if they did not listen to even bigger worries about a single currency. Far from creating harmony and peace in Europe, the single currency plan would reawaken tensions and disagreements as well as damaging our prosperity. It is an experiment we cannot afford and must not inflict on countries already damaged by unemployment bred of convergence. Let's trade together, co-operate where we can, build friendships. Let's not pretend that sharing a currency is a technical matter, or that it would help business. It is a fundamental constitutional issue. Abolishing the pound would be a grave mistake.

A Global Vision

A speech delivered to the CBI conference by The Rt. Hon.
John Redwood, MP, Birmingham, November 14th 1995

It is time to save Europe from itself.

I want a prosperous and strong Europe. A Europe that looks
forward, not one that looks back. Britain must speak out for policies
that will bring more jobs and business. We must speak for a Britain
in Europe and a Europe in the world that can bring greater economic
success. We have no need to be afraid of our involvement in Europe,
and no reason to suppress our true views. Britain's global view has
never been more needed.

Every year in the run up to the Budget, the CBI give the
Chancellor their advice on how he should adjust the levers of the
British economy. It is a healthy part of our democratic process. The
Chancellor listens. He decides the balance between the different
viewpoints and pressure groups. He can decide to change interest
rates, increase or decrease borrowing, change public spending as he
sees fit.

He could no longer do this if Britain joins a single currency. There
would be no pound and no interest rate for the Chancellor to set.
Our £25000m of National Savings, our foreign exchange reserves,
would move to Frankfurt. They would pass out of our control to
support the new currency. Interest rates and lending policies would
be decided by unelected officials in Frankfurt. There would be little
point in the CBI lobbying them. Taxes would be driven by the need
to send money to the weaker parts of the European Union. The
central bank would control how much we can borrow.

Liverpool and London live in one country with a single currency.
The richer parts of London pay higher taxes to subsidise Liverpool.
Taxpayers accept the obligation as the price of being one nation, one
extended family. Would we feel the same about paying higher taxes
to look after Sicily or Eastern Germany? That is what would be
expected of us. If we did not like it or felt the rates were too high,
there would be very little we could do about it.

In 1990, opposing entry into the Exchange rate mechanism was
heretic-speak. It was one of those times when politicians, business

leaders and the media mirrored each other's assertions until joining the ERM became 'inevitable'. They said it would usher in the golden scenario. Instead interest rates had to be kept high. Businesses went bust. A million jobs were lost. Our foreign exchange reserves were used in defending the pound.

The Exchange Rate Mechanism was a warning. Every currency fell out of the narrow bands against the DM. If some of the strain had not been taken on the currencies, more of the strain would have been taken in factory closures and lost jobs. As it was, our attempts to stay in - attempts urged on by Labour and many economists - cost British business dear.

Who wants to go back to the level of interest rates it took to keep up with the DM? A single currency would be a permanent ERM. None of the strain could be taken on the exchange rate. All of the strain would be taken on profits, turnover and jobs. Of course people would like to be free of foreign exchange commissions, but surely not at the price of losing competitiveness or closing down ?

London is one of the big three financial centres of the world. More overseas banks congregate in London than in any other centre. German style banking regulation from Frankfurt would change all that. Foreign banks might decide that the new capital and business controls made it no longer worthwhile staying in Europe. Others might decide that moving closer to the Regulator was sensible. Without doubt London would be the loser.

When Britain came off the Gold Standard between the wars an era of prosperity began. It took many years to repair all the damage of fixed exchange rates. The continental countries that remain in the new wide band ERM need to come out. Spanish and French companies could then compete better. Their unemployment would come down more quickly relieved of the burden of following German monetary policy.

But what of larger companies salivating at the thought of fewer currency transactions? Well, most that I know of buy hard and soft commodities in dollars, they buy oil and gas in dollars, they buy many imported components in dollars. They would still have substantial exchange risk and dealing costs between ecus and dollars. Indeed, if minimising transactions costs is really the aim, perhaps Britain should abolish the pound and join the dollar.

In practise, big business can manage its affairs through a common rather than a single currency, and through foreign exchange forward markets. When I chaired an industrial PLC I did not take undue foreign exchange risks. Running a global company, it was not the cost of foreign exchange dealing that occupied most of my hours. I certainly never wanted a single European currency then, nor membership of the ERM.

If we entered a single currency, business would soon discover that far from making it easier for them, it had made them uncompetitive.

Don't be a sheep and be exported live into Europe against your will. First think through the single currency for your business. Ask what effect it would have on all your other costs, not just the exchange costs.

So where am I coming from? Am I just a little Englander looking back to golden years past? Certainly not. My vision for the future is a global one - Great Britain in a great world. This country lives and prospers by trading the world, not just Europe. The sinews of our manufactures and the strength of our services earn us our living. We have a powerful interest in a prosperous and growing European Community. We have mighty interests in Asia and America. There is a distinctive British interest. It is often an interest which is good for others in the world. It is based upon our belief in free trade and democracy, buttressed by our defence of the right of peoples to self-determination and human rights. It is vital that we find as many allies and supporters as we can, in the four corners of the world, for our ideals.

A recent CBI survey has reaffirmed how members see the importance of European trade to our success. It also shows that members think Britain was right to say 'No' to the Social Chapter, which would have undermined jobs here at home. It shows that many companies now see Asia as the fastest growing continent. They see the Far East as the most important centre for new investment. Politicians should ask themselves why so many businesses are now voting with their cheque books for Asia rather than Europe?

Today I want to set out a positive agenda for Britain in Europe, to attempt to wrestle back some of the growth and excitement to our own continent. I want Britain to wield an influence that does justice to our history as a foremost defender of freedom, and does justice to our belief that free trade is the best engine of prosperity. Britain does not need to punch above her weight. She needs to remember she has weight. Our weight comes from inherited moral authority that standing for something in the world has brought through the centuries. It comes from the justice of our cause.

In a few weeks time at Madrid, and a few months time at the IGC, Britain has a unique opportunity to change and mould the putty of Community policy. We must warn Europe, before it is too late, that European policy is not working. Europe is not working. 1 in 5 are out of work in Spain. 1 in 7 are out of work in Ireland. 1 in 8 are out of work in France. The dole queues have been lengthening. In Japan, said to be in recession, less than 1 in 30 are unemployed.

We should say at Madrid that the people of Europe want a Europe that works. We should be positive. More jobs can come in Europe. Unemployment need not be permanently higher than 1 in 10.

The European Community should:

— Speed negotiations with Eastern Europe to bring down more trade barriers.

— Cut the burden of regulation on EC companies by repealing those many Directives that seek to control product design and limit innovation.

— Roll back state subsidies which tilt the playing field against British companies and whole industries like steel.

— Begin to negotiate a common market of the North Atlantic

— Recognise that Europe is overburdened with taxation, the costs of overgovernment, and begin to rein in the EC budget.

It is time for business to work with government to get over these basic truths:

— That Britain is a leading progenitor and proponent of a common market.

— That Europe is not ready for a Single Currency.

— That preparations for a single currency are doing grave damage to business and jobs.

— That Europe must turn all its energies to making itself open and friendly to business.

— That Europe belongs in a global marketplace, which will teem with opportunity and competitive challenge.

— That wealth has to be earned before it can be taxed or redistributed.

— That jobs come from customers not from governments.

At home government must also heed business voices. Cutting costs in business is important. The costs government imposes on business are many times the cost of foreign exchange dealing. It is those that the governments of Western Europe should be agonising over. Despite cutting interest rates by more than half since leaving the ERM, business conditions for many, especially in property and construction, remain difficult. A government which believes in deregulation is still enacting far too many rules and regulations. The City is being stifled by rule books. The fishing industry is being hit by the Common Fisheries Policy. Private care homes are being undermined by Labour Councils that won't use them for ideological reasons. Business is difficult enough, without all these unhelpful hands.

Surely we can persuade our partners that throwing back dead fish into the sea does nothing to conserve fish? Can't we see that financial clients want to be protected against theft: they don't want to pay extra for more regulators and less choice? Surely we can shame Labour Councils into using better private sector homes that are often cheaper as well? Does it have to be a criminal offence if someone is prepared to sell me a pound of sausages?

All too often regulation is a heavy sledgehammer to miss a nut. The reign of the mad official needs to be brought to an end. Depose him before we have lost too many jobs and good ideas.

I am optimistic about British business prospects if we can keep government under control. I am pessimistic about Mr. Blair's approach to these matters. He has no fight to stand up for jobs and business against European rules and regulations. Signing the social chapter will destroy jobs and drive up costs. When did Mr Blair or his party last criticise a Euro-rule or suggest we would be better off not signing? Indeed, Mr Blair's stated policy is to give in before negotiating. He says Britain should never be isolated. Imagine him negotiating for your company with a supplier. He would go to the supplier and ask him what he wanted to supply and how much it would cost. He would then say thank you and accept. He wouldn't want to be isolated. In your business he wouldn't get the job.

He is equally naive about the single currency. Does he realise that the Europe-wide deflation on the continent has been caused by the preparations for the single currency? Does he care about European unemployment? Does he agree with his own Deputy, John Prescott, that a minimum wage would cause job losses? Does he care about that? Where does he think all the jobs and apprenticeships he rightly wants will come from, if we signed the Social Chapter, adopted a minimum wage and re-entered the ERM to prepare for a single currency? I don't believe he is as heartless as his policies. I can only presume he has failed to think them through. By trying to be nice, he has been naive. His naivety would cost many in Britain their jobs, if ever translated into action.

If government does the right things, prospects for British business are good. We are strong in those very areas that are going to grow rapidly in the world markets of tomorrow. We are good at pharmaceuticals, telecommunications,multi-media, financial and business services. We are fast rebuilding our position in motor car design and manufacture. We are good at defence and aviation engineering. Wherever we have had the courage of our conviction - government to deregulate and industry to innovate - we have done well. We have gone from backwater to a world leader in telecommunications in a decade. We have changed from non-runner to front-runner in satellite and cable media in less than a decade. We have gone from a joke to being a serious medium sized competitor in cars in ten years.

Britain can make it. It is often better made in Britain. Let's show Europe we are committed to winning in Europe and the wider world. And let's set out a programme to save Europe from mass unemployment. That way we could have real influence - for good.

Arguments against a single European currency

by Hywel Williams

The project of a single European currency is a political one. It arises out of contemporary European politics, from the wishes, fears and insecurities of the European political class who use economic arguments in order to advance the goal of political union. Sceptics point out that monetary union could only follow and reflect political union. Currencies follow the flag and should not be manipulated to serve a political dream. Britain is an independent country; the pound is no mere symbol, but part of the warp and woof of a nation state whose economic policies are adapted to the particular and varying needs of the British people. If, at some future date, Britain's political independence were lost, the demise of the pound would be the consequence of that melancholy event.

Europhiliacs differ. Addicted to an ideological Utopianism alien to the political British tradition, they dream dreams of an united European State. At the same time they know that Europe's political diversity is so great that political union will only arrive very slowly - if at all. A timetable must therefore be invented and economics, the hand maid of politics, must be press-ganged into service, take the commissioners' Ecu and accomplish the political goal which politics, left to its own, would fail to accomplish. Establish a common European Currency and a common European political order will follow as night follows day.

Sceptics observe that the political consequences of monetary union would be disastrous for Britain and would entail the loss of British independence. They also doubt whether Britain is an European economy at all. The politician who voted for the pound's abolition would become a member of a redundant species. He would have no legitimate say on policies affecting inflation, employment, and economic growth. Why should he bother to stand for election to the House of Commons? The words of his election address would be hollow when he pontificated on his country's economic future, for he would be without influence.

Proponents of monetary union in Britain rarely avow their political goals explicitly. Knowing the power and the depth of popular instinct against their views they prefer stealth. Monetary union is then presented as a mere technical matter. Crude bullying hysteria in favour of EMU is more often heard on the continental mainland. Chancellor Kohl has appeared to suggest that it is Europe's political destiny to save Germany from herself - to be the good democratic angel to the bad angel of the totalitarian past and its long shadow. Addressing his party's annual congress on October 16th 1995, Mr Kohl said 'There is no alternative for us to a free and unified Germany within a free and unified Europe'. The 1925 Locarno Pact had created the illusion of permanent peace, which was shattered within eight years. History would catch up with the men of Maastricht as it did with the men of Locarno - unless European Union was embraced as an 'irreversible process for which the decisive steps will follow in the next two years'. The European union needed a permanently integrated economic and finance policy in order to achieve currency union. Otherwise Yugoslavia's descent into mass rape, ethnic cleansing, and murder could spread to a whole continent.

Mr Kohl's remarks betray the gulf between most British Tories and most continental politicians in their view of what 'Europe' is for. Centralising supernational institutions can seem an escape route for countries whose domestic history in the first half of the twentieth century was disastrous and savage. British Tories keen on responsibility and freedom in the affairs of nations and those of individuals, see this as an evasion of duty. The problems of Berlin and Paris, of Rome and Madrid, will not become less acute when seen through Brussels spectacles - however rose-tinted. Indeed, the history of the EMU debate shows how 'pro-European' arguments are a cause of European conflict not of harmony and of peace. When an EU official, Mr Bernard Connolly, made this elementary point and warned of possible future conflict, he was vilified by the Europhiliacs. Ancestral voices prophesying war should, it seems, be confined to those like Mr Kohl, who use that threat for integrationist purposes.

44

The politics of the European Union are those of adolescence. Born in the Cold War, the institutions have yet to adapt to the adult global economy, where markets are deregulated, the government fallacy is on the retreat and the individual has more choice. Fear of the freedom of this new world has led to insecurity, posturing and protectionist temper tantrums. Arguments continue late into the night in the chancelleries of Europe with much imputation of bad faith and accusations of a refusal to understand. EMU will have to be abandoned before Europe can enter the adult world of economic modernity.

Europe needs jobs and has to be more competitive. EMU and its accompanying common economic policies for Europe will fail to achieve those ends. Currencies need to cover geographical areas where economic activity is broadly similar and/or where there is a continuity of political will, a political tradition and purpose. Europe's economies, however, are diverse. An economic crisis to be managed by an European macro-economic policy would have widely differing effects. Some parts would be badly affected, others much less so. The same economic policy proscription - higher interest rates say - could be, at the same time, inappropriate to the unaffected areas and weak beer for the afflicted. Exchange rates offset a crude pan-continental response, the rate can rise and fall according to the country's needs, as can interest rates. Monetary union, however, means that all European union would face the same level of interest rates.

Geography and politics determine the maximum effective area to be covered by a single currency. The larger the area the greater the variety of economic forms of life , the more varied the impact of economic cycles and the greater the need to react to those cycles by exchange rate changes.

This is a more fundamental truth than the marginal benefits of getting rid of the costs of currency transactions within EMU. We no longer expect politicians to run our economy but we do hold them accountable for economic policies. At the moment we can praise them or blame them. Under EMU we could do neither which doubtless appeals to politicians who wish to escape responsibility. Part of the appeal of Europe to the political class is that the buck can always be passed.

Political facts have to underline an area of common currency. The United States, for example, contains wide economic diversity within its political borders. It is possible to conceive of Texas and California having their own currencies. But politics has long since disposed of that possibility in American history. Europhiliacs would like a similar disposal in European history, but there can be no economic analogy between the USA and the EMU model. The flexibility of the American economy enables it to adapt to economic adversity and prosperity. No Brussels style directives on wages and conditions of work issue from Washington. That is a contrast which is set to widen with the European Union social chapter, the social action programme and directives such as the Posted Workers and Working Time directives.

In the United States, as in Britain, economic policies and taxation reflect political allegiance. The South-East subsidises Liverpool. That is done because Kentish man and the Liverpudlian share an identity as Britons, as subjects of the Queen. Europhiliacs wish the European Union to acquire a similar political identity - an identity which would allow vast transfers of wealth to take place between different parts of Europe. Such transfers already take place - as those who have driven on Greek motorways can testify. There is no common European political allegiance which would tolerate a further extension of such fiscal transfers. It is, however, exactly that web of allegiance which EMU is designed to develop. Without it, EMU entails destructive pan-european economic policies. Europhiliacs know this — which is why the social dimension to Europe exists in order to alleviate those consequences. Fiscal transfers, however, on this scale, would ensure that Europe remains in the rigid corporatist post-war world which spawned the Community's institutions. That is a world in which the efficient exist in order to subsidise the inefficient, a world which penalises success and pauperises the dependent, a continent fit for graft, subsidy and venality.

At the heart of EMU lies the question of the Bank. Here Tory habits of scepticism, suspicion of theory and reverence for experience become most marked. Franco-German quarrels and reconciliations are the motor of the European union. Each country has a different view of the bank it wants. For the Germans the ideal bank would be another version of the Bundesbank. For the French, monetary union would actually be a way of escaping the franc's chronic linkage with the Deutschmark. We are invited to step into a morass of confused aims, to jettison over three hundred years of experience of the Bank of England and a far longer history of the Exchequer's control over our currency.

The argument that EMU would benefit trade as a result of getting rid of exchange rate fluctuations has more relevance to continental European economies than to our own. Our total trade with the EU in goods, services and invisible earnings, is far less than our trade with the rest of the world. Even with a single currency, therefore, a very high proportion of British trade will still involve a currency exchange. Savings have been estimated at no more than 0.2% of GDP per annum. Even this figure assumes that the fifteen EU members will qualify and wish to join in EMU in 1999. There is little likelihood, however, that Greece, Portugal, Spain, Italy and Sweden will meet the convergence criteria. Belgium, Finland, Ireland and the Netherlands will only meet modified versions of the criteria.

Only 47% of Britain's trade is with EU countries. In 1993 these companies accounted for 57% of Britain's exported goods and 55% of her imported goods. Invisible trades such as services, however, are of fundamental importance to the British economy. In 1993 the EU accounted for only 36.3% of Britain's invisible exports and 36.7 % of her invisible imports. If the picture is confined to the core EU countries of Germany, France, the Netherlands, Austria and Belgium the conclusions are even more striking. Less than a third of Britain's total visible and invisible exports and imports is with these countries.

A similar picture is true of investment patterns. In 1993 UK companies' investment in core EU countries amounted to only 30% of total overseas investment, 16.3% of investment to the UK in the same year came from those core countries. Exchange rate variability is, in other words, a fact of life for the British economy. Eliminating that uncertainty for part of our trade would result in our entanglement in an European economy fuelled by subsidy and protectionism.

A single currency is not necessary in order to secure the single market. The North-American free trade agreement incorporates the United States, Canada and Mexico as a free trade area but without establishing a single North American currency. The same should be true of the European free trade area. Intra-EC flows of trade and investment tend to be long term matters. They are not easily disrupted by exchange rate variability. Indeed, a report commissioned by the Commission itself came to the conclusion that it could find no relationship between such variability and flows of trade and investment within the European community.

The independence of an European Central Bank is regarded by many as an important and redeeming attribute but, on present form, the Bank will not be so much independent as autocratic and unaccountable, its workings beyond democratic control and its bureaucracy and policies beyond the scrutiny of nation states. It seems clear that the Bank's existence would provide an excuse for further European integrationist measures and institutions which would develop policies and goals for the Bank. The day could not be far off when a European bank, and those who ran it, would choose to intervene in the domestic taxation issues of the nation states.

The more one looks at the British economy the more striking its distinction from the economies of other European countries. Only the Netherlands competes with it as a major producer of oil and gas. Financial services and media sectors are much more developed in Britain. Our international trading position means that the exchange rate between the Ecu and the dollar would always be of fundamental importance. Our economy reflects our values. Britons are home owners and household debt is correspondingly high. Interest payments as a proportion of income amount to 10.9% in Britain compared to 3.9% in France and 3.2% in Germany.

Even if monetary union, therefore, did establish price and employment stability in other European countries, it could not do so in Britain. A rise in interest rates in order to achieve that end would always have a disproportionate effect on the British economy and household incomes because of our investment in variable rate mortgages and comparative lack of interest bearing assets.

Participation in EMU would undermine the City of London's position as one of the three world financial centres with New York and Tokyo. There are some three hundred and fifty non-UK banks represented in London. Two thirds of these have a non-EU base. The City's reach with a favourable regulatory and tax regime is global. Business is growing fast on the Pacific rim and in the heart of Europe. EMU could lead to European restrictions on financial services and a reduction in the substantial services they earn for the British balance of payments. Inward investment in the United

48

Kingdom is substantial. We received in 1992 43.6% of all EU inward investment. Investors come to Britain because of good communications, skilled labour, low non-wage labour costs and the English language. EMU would increase labour costs and destabilise the British economy thereby reducing Britain's attraction to the investor.

Europhiliacs prophesy Britain's loss of influence if she remained outside EMU. They are wrong. Britain's contribution to Europe will be that of a paradigm. She will show how an independent monetary policy, with a deregulated market and a realistic and a deregulated exchange rate can operate successfully within a competitive global economy. The alternative is an accelerated involvement in a flawed political project characterised by dishonest presentation, sclerotic bureaucracy and an antediluvian faith in government's redemptive powers.

Twenty years ago the people of Britain voted to join a Common Market. They were told that there would be no political consequences and that the independence of their country would be unaffected. In 1995 they know that 'Europeanism' is tearing the heart out of Europe. Twenty years ago they were subjected to the risible sight of European high culture, of Beethoven and Bach, of Goethe and Racine, of Titian and Tintoretto, being press-ganged posthumously as the apostles of Brussels. In 1995 we know that this was a hollow gesture and that the cause of a centralised Europe is that of a corrupt and elitist bureaucracy. If they could vote again they would vote for a free exchange of goods and service - but not for the untrammelled growth of government which has issued from Brussels.

The fall of the Berlin Wall prompted some to talk of 'the end of history'. 1989 was certainly a victory for the principle of free markets over command economies. It showed how liberty was indivisible and that free markets have democratic consequences. But the 1990s have shown the continuing, destabilising, power of ideology in the European political class. The project of a politically centralised Europe has replaced the forces of the Warsaw Pact as a threat to European political order and good sense. As our economies became more global so it will be necessary for European peoples to continue to claim their homes as their own, to retain their sense of identity. Nationalism in its racist and ideological form destroyed 20th century Europe - but the task of the wise politician is to understand and work with its grain. When ignored or denied nationalism acquires a virulent strain. When European people feel that their governments lack legitimacy, that they are remote from their interests and concerns, that their governors have more in common with each other then they do with those whom they rule: that is the moment of danger and the opportunity for demagogues.

Britain has had for three centuries a national identity without the ideological nationalism which infected some continental countries from the late 19th century onwards. Its institutions are astonishingly long-lived. 'Independent'- reading sceptics may scoff at the 'invention of traditions', at ceremonies re-discovered and packaged for the 20th century mass democracy. It remains true that this country united early and successfully while Teutonic princelings and French parlements squabbled and killed. The sovereignty of an institution, of the Crown in Parliament, lay at the heart of the British success story. It was the Parliament of 1690-95 which finally established the legislature's distinctive questioning powers of the executive. Exported to a new world as the doctrine of the division of powers, admired and imitated throughout the Empire and Commonwealth, envied by European commentators such as Voltaire and Montesquieu mired in the age of absolutism - that constitutional innovation has done more to advance freedom than any European legal code in the Napoleonic model.

Thomas Cromwell's words in his preamble to the Act of Appeals (1533) echo across the centuries:

'This realm of England is an Empire, and so hath been accepted in the world, governed by one Supreme Head and King having the dignity and royal estate of the imperial Crown of the same, unto whom a body politic, compact of all sorts and degrees of people divided in terms and by names of Spirituality and Temporalty, be bounden and owe to bear next to God a natural and humble obedience.'

A sense of identity requires an institutional home, it has to be anchored in place, time and history. Parliament retains its hold as an institution in the affections of the British people - however disillusioned they may be about the conduct of individual members. It has given body and substance to what it means to be British - and it has shown how debates can be real without bloodshed. By its side the debates in the French National Assembly and the Bundestag appear mere shadow-boxing, an elaborate and bloodless ballet between contestants whose real desire is to gratify government. National identity only becomes dangerous when it is denied institutional life and seeks refuge in abstraction, racist mysticism and agonising about 'heimat'.

The British political tradition has always prided itself in its lack of ideology, its pragmatism and coolness towards doctrine. The events of 1640-1660 were a rebellion, a breakdown of order - rather than a revolution - and served only to strengthen a native antipathy towards doctrinal politics. Our closest European neighbours are the Swiss.

The irruption of Brussels into our affairs, however, is an ideological infection. It has the power of an idea which thinks its moment has come - and its neophytes brook neither argument nor contradiction. Criticism is dismissed as the cry of the eccentric. That is why 1989 was not a lasting victory for liberal democracy. Statism survives in new forms. Belief in a European superstate is the secular version of Marxism. Like Marxism it thinks it marches with the big battalions and seeks to convince by force of numbers rather than force of argument. Like Marxism, it is heedless of evidence and resistant to refutation. Like Marxism, it asserts the inevitability of its proposed scheme of human improvement. Its bounds shall be set wider still and wider within a corporatist framework of state intervention, subsidy and hostility to the extra-European world.

There was a time when the Labour Party, though misguided in other spheres, was patriotic. Bevin and Bevan cared for freedom and for Britain. Their successors, however, have found in European Christian Democracy a means of satisfying socialism's regulatory impulses in a post-1989 world. Methodism without Marx has joined hands with Papal Encyclicals on the rights of labour. It is a world which is keener on the rights of groups rather than of individuals, and on the solidarity of association rather than the freedom of the subject. 'Europe' has been the newspeak by which new Labour has packaged old socialism for a new world.

The consequences of a single currency, therefore, would be a destabilizing concentration of power. Constitutionally, our country has shown the world that power divided is power legitimized and scrutinized. Diplomatically, its security is bound up with the balance of power. A concentration of power on the European mainland deprives Britain of an essential platform in the defence of its permanent interests. Newspeak tells us that European integration is a path to peace. Experience has shown that the road to hell is paved with good intentions. Preparing the superstate is wrecking Europe. It has created an European recession worse than at any time since the 1930s. It has ensured the return of the dole-queue to the European streets. Corrupt and inefficient accounting systems lead European people to be ever more resentful and cynical about their governors.

At the end of one great European war the younger Pitt observed that his country had 'saved herself by her exertions and Europe by her example.' The 50th anniversary of the end of another war which called forth a similar exertion and example is a good time for reflection. Britain has always been for European thinkers the model of how to combine a liberal political order with economic progress. It has shown how material advance does not arrive by the fiat of princes or the dictats of magistrates - but by the energies of a free people. It has illustrated how pride in country need not lead to rancorous ideologies of race. Its unity has been compatible with the cultural varieties of English, Welsh, Scots and Irish. Britain brings to the European party a sophisticated awareness that the successful politician goes with, and not against, the grain of his country's history, genius and traditions. 'The grounds of government are not so easily washed away' said Clarendon in the middle of one constitutional disaster - and so it proved. Britain must continue to defend her interest in Europe by extending her influence. She must continue to punch her weight. Her democratic picture of free trade and good government is what Europe needs to avoid disaster at the hands of those who would force us all into the same Procrustean bed and turn out the lights.

Engines of State

by Andrew Roberts

"The stability of the Bank of England is equal to that of the British Government", wrote Adam Smith in *The Wealth of Nations*: "It acts, not only as an ordinary bank, but as a great engine of state"(1). Since the Middle Ages, central banks and treasuries have acted as engines of state, primarily through their administration of currency. Although some people, such as the British Chancellor of the Exchequer, Kenneth Clarke, have long denied that the creation of a European Central Bank controlling a European single currency would necessarily have profound constitutional implications for the individual nations' sovereignty, historical precedent totally contradicts them.

Not only have empires almost always used single currencies to promote political hegemony, but also the very creation of such currencies has very often actually been the vehicle for the creation of the superstates themselves. The incidence of unitary monetary policy being employed by superstates (or would-be superstates) is so marked in every past age that it cannot be mere coincidence. Nor is there any reason to suppose that the European Union would baulk at behaving in the same way in the future.

Empires and federations naturally tend to deploy the politically unifying power of single currencies to further their non-economic aims. Indeed such is the tenacity some imperial currencies possess that they can even outlive their creators. Gold napoleons were in use long after their eponymous creator died on St. Helena, and a shilling comprised twenty denarii over fifteen centuries after the last Roman soldier left Britain.

Superstates have long appreciated how a common currency acts both as a symptom of and a spur to centralised power. Conversely, control over monetary policy - and there is no more tangible sign of control than the authority to mint and distribute coinage - is a sure sign of continued political sovereignty. As one distinguished historian has recently commented: "Running your own currency is the ultimate test of whether you are independent and free". (2)

EARLY HISTORY

The word Sterling derives from 'easterlings' or 'esterlingi' the Saxon traders who first regulated the English coinage. Two hundred and forty pennies then weighed a pound of silver, so the pound sterling has been unit of currency since even before the creation of the nation state itself. Marks replaced the local Saxon currency at the Norman Conquest, after William I established a mint at the Tower of London. It was the last time in British history that a currency was imposed from abroad.

It was not until 1352, in the reign of Edward III, that an Act was passed declaring that all coinage had to be made government-specified, Sterling standards. That monarch, the first to speak English as his chosen language, needed to be able to regulate his taxation and tributes in order to pursue a ruthlessly hegemonic series of wars against his Irish, French and Scots neighbours. His reign has been described as the period in which "the England of our own day began to be formed". (3) Financially rapacious, Edward managed to squeeze grants out of his parliaments which lasted two or in some cases three years, enabling him to rule largely through ordinance and in council, rather than by parliamentary statute. It is a recurring theme that tight central control over the exchequer often stifles representative government, let alone democracy.

Although evidence of central banks and treasuries, with clay tablets showing money-lending, financial advances and balances, have been discovered in Babylonia and Assyria - both imperial powers in their day - the first modern bank was the Banco di Rialto, established in Venice by senatorial acts in 1584 and 1587. It aided the massive expansion of Venetian commerce in the Mediterranean and beyond. In 1619 the Banco del Giro was founded, which became the only public bank allowed in the state. By 1797, when Napoleon invaded Italy, it was considered such a threat to French interests that it was closed. Central banks have always been deeply political institutions, and, however much the European Commissioners of tomorrow promise a 'hands-off' approach, they will always remain so.

The imperialism of Philip II of Spain found an assiduous propagandist in the Piedmontese failed Jesuit Giovanni Botero. It was he who penned the famous sentence that for Spain: "Territory is acquired a little at a time but it must be preserved together as a whole". To achieve this, as he wrote in his 'Delle Ragioni di Stato' ('On the Reasons of State'), the Spanish Empire would require a single language, a single currency and a single body of customs in order that "subjects acquired by conquest may come to resemble natural subjects". (4) Thankfully, Sir Francis Drake saw off this particular attempt to impose a single European currency.

THE NAPOLEONIC THREAT

On 13th June 1800 the First Consul of the French Republic, Napoleon Bonaparte, founded the Bank of France. It was distinguished from earlier French banks by, as one history describes, "its intimate relations with the government". Napoleon himself, his family and other high officers of state took shares in it, and after its share capital was greatly increased in April 1803 it was granted the exclusive privilege of issuing bank-notes. (5) Banks which had hitherto enjoyed this privilege either went under or were bought out by the Bank of France. Over the following twelve years Napoleon used the Bank unashamedly as an "engine of state" in his quest for European territorial and financial acquisition. It was partly the Bank of England's power and probity, especially during the period of Napoleon's Continental System blockade of British trade, which saw Britain through its darkest moment of peril until 1940.

The Bank of France's constitution, written by Napoleon's banker M. Perrigeaux, is financial dirigisme at its Bonapartist best. The provisions for managing all government loans and centralising tax collection were hugely aided by Napoleon's command of the minting and issuing of currency. This was something that Revolutionary France had never hitherto managed to master, indeed there were more illegal currency dealers guillotined during the Terror than there were aristos.

The franc itself had been a unit of French currency since a gold coin was minted in 1360 bearing the effigy of King John II on horseback, with the words 'Johannes Dei Gracia Francorum Rex'. Since the invention of metal coinage, issuing authorities have used currency as a propaganda tool. Roman emperors, fascist dictators and modern constitutional monarchs have all had their names and faces on the currency. Those ecus which are already in circulation are equally shameless in their promotion of the images of European unity. A country's currency helps define it; archaeologists can deduce huge amounts about a culture from its numismatics. Coinage, like the central banks which mints it, is thus always political, because he who ultimately controls it is sovereign. Simultaneously with the abolition of the pound sterling must come the end of British sovereignty.

CENTRAL BANKS

Soon after the Bank of Amsterdam was founded in 1609 it became "the heart that pumped the bloodstream of Dutch commerce". (6) It was instrumental through its introduction of new methods of regulating the exchange of foreign currencies and of minting coins of fixed rate and value - i.e. by the piecemeal introduction of a single currency and exchange rate mechanism - in rendering the guilder the most powerful currency of the seventeenth century. Between 1619 and 1820 the Bank of Amsterdam, in the words of one history, worked "in the assistance of commerce not by loans but by the local manufacture, so to speak, of an international currency".(7)

The Bank was also instrumental in supporting the Dutch campaign for independence from Spain, which was eventually won in 1648. The single currency helped unify the state. Its power and stability - more than half of European trade was denominated in guilders by the mid-seventeenth century - gave the Dutch the confidence and ability to put ten thousand ships to sea, sail up the Medway, and buy Manhattan and other important bases in both the East and West Indies. For a homogenous state yearning for freedom, therefore, a single currency can be as potent and positive a force for nationalism as it can be a hazard for heterogeneous entities, such as today's European Union.

It is no coincidence that the creation of the Bank of England on 27th July 1694 followed the Glorious Revolution, which had been supported by Whig merchants who wanted a Protestant, stable, parliamentary state from which to trade. For that they required both William of Orange and a solid bank from which the not-so-solid Revolutionary ministry could borrow. As Adam Smith pointed out: "The credit of the new government, established by the Revolution...must have been very low when it was obliged to borrow at so high an interest". Only four years had passed since the Battle of the Boyne and the London government was forced to pay 8% for

56

its initial 1.2 million loan. After the Act of Union, however, the Bank considered the regime secure enough in 1708 to lend at the 6% rate usually charged to individuals. (8)

The Bank's relative stability - it was founded by William Patterson, a Scot - was a key factor in persuading Lowland Scottish commercial interests to embrace political union. The Scots continued to set up note-issuing private banks until 1844, but gradually the greater acceptability of the Bank's paper meant that the Union came generally to be seen as good for business north of the border. Sir Robert Peel's Bank Charter Acts of 1844 and 1845 established the existing system of note issue in the United Kingdom. They, along with the Free Trade policies the Peelites pursued, helped create a new financial stability which enabled entrepreneurial Scottish cities such as Dundee to make their mark on the Empire.

It was only after the Bank was nationalised in 1945 that day-to-day political considerations were allowed to impinge on the traditional low-inflation, strong-Sterling objectives of the Governor and Court. The Scottish experience suggests that political union can be allied with monetary union, but only if both countries perceive it in their own interests. The Jacobite Revolts of 1715 and 1745 notwithstanding, most Scots supported the Union, which had anyway been a form of constitutional reverse-takeover since James I had been King of Scotland before succeeding Elizabeth I over a century before. The equivalent of the Scottish success of 1603 and 1707 would be today's European Union countries swearing allegiance to Queen Elizabeth II as their Head of State.

A nation wishing for independence, as was seen in mid-seventeenth century Holland, soon seizes control of the currency. In 1781, during the American War of Independence, the respected merchant Robert Morris set up the Bank of North America, winning a charter from the rebel state of Pennsylvania the following year. Congress elected Morris Superintendent of Finance, and he can claim to be one of America's true Revolutionary heroes. It was partly his banking genius, commercial contacts and leadership qualities which provided George Washington with the financial wherewithal to halt desertion, increase recruitment and go onto the military offensive. (9) It was also he who, with Washington, commissioned Betty Ross to sew the first Stars and Stripes flag. No better example can be imagined than this of a nationalist financier creating national identity.

Although the Confederate States of America attempted to establish a separate currency after secession in 1861, it was Lincoln's Mr Secretary Chase of the Union Treasury who won the financial Civil War by introducing the 'greenback' dollar in 1862. The Union's ability to secure its currency helped it to finance the cripplingly expensive struggle. Confederate paper currency and war loans were rendered worthless after the surrender at Appromatox, ruining vast swathes of the population overnight and illustrating the pitfalls which any unsuccessful secessionist movement must face. Certainly, any attempt to leave the European single currency once it was established would face almost insuperable difficulties, especially if the (by then presumably defunct) Bank of England's specie reserves had been removed.

BISMARCK AND AN EARLIER UNION

In 1865 France, Italy, Switzerland and Belgium formed the Latin Monetary Union, an ill-fated attempt to protect their gold and silver-based - 'bimetallic' - currencies from Germany and the incursions of the vast amounts of gold which had been flooding the market since the Australian and Californian Gold Rushes of the late 1840s. In a classically European and dirigiste attempt to buck the world market, the four countries, soon joined by Greece, Serbia and Romania, agreed to fix the amount of silver which could be minted annually, so as to manage the relative appreciation of silver vis à vis gold. They also agreed to follow the franc into decimalisation.

This scheme soon fell foul of the Germans, who operated a gold-based coinage. When after 1870 gold production diminished and silver production increased enormously, the newly-unified German Empire struck. In 1873 they sold silver and bought gold on a massive scale, whilst also demanding reparations from the Franco-Prussian War to be paid in gold. The Latin Union attempted to suspend the coinage of silver altogether in order to protect stocks, but it was soon forced into what historians call "limping", or incomplete, bimetallism, leaving the new Reich victorious.

In 1875 Bismarck created the Reichsbank, merging it with the Bank of Prussia the following year. According to its constitution, the Imperial Chancellor appointed its President and council, directed its policy and ensured a proportion of its annual profits went to the Imperial Treasury. As a gesture towards subsidiarity, the state banks of Saxony, Bavaria and Württemberg were allowed to issue notes, but only in tiny amounts to be governed strictly by Berlin. It became a classic "engine of state" for the consolidation and eventual enlargement of the Wilhelmine Empire.

Bismarck had early on spotted the potential of the Zollverein (customs union) as a vehicle for German unification. He used commercial treaties and trade pressures almost as war by other means. Whenever they failed, or even stalled, he opted for the real thing. In 1858 a congress of German economists agitated for a single German currency. Bismarck could see the political implications of this for Prussia, if only the Austrians could be marginalised. The next year saw the Deutsche Nationalverein (German National Society), a group of nationalist businessmen, intellectuals and junkers, call for Prussia to lead the unification process. All Bismarck had to do was connect the economic with the political movements, which he did expertly. By 1861 the economists had set up an all-Germany chamber of commerce, the Handelstag, which in turn spawned the Zollverein. When it was renewed for twelve years in October 1864, Bismarck ensured that Austria, in alliance with whom he had just defeated the Danes, was excluded.

By the summer of 1867, after Austria had itself been defeated by Prussia in a six week war ending in the Battle of Sadowa, the Zollverein members unanimously placed the management of their trade and economic affairs in the hands of the North German Confederation, which was dominated by Prussia. A committee of its legislature swiftly created the Zollbundersrath (federal tariff council) and the Zollparlement (customs parliament). As far as the smaller, Catholic, semi-independent, economically-backward, southern German states were concerned, "the economic disadvantages of this innovation were obvious, but it was of political consequence, on the other hand, that subjects of all the states of Germany met in a single council, and that German people grew accustomed to receiving the impulse from Berlin in one important branch of public life". (11)

Contrary to what the south-west Germans had hoped, after the Empire was proclaimed in the Versailles Hall of Mirrors on 18th January 1871, Germany actually became more Prussian in outlook and ambition, rather than less. The implications for today's economic-cum-political European customs union, which is increasingly receiving its own "impulse from Berlin", are obvious.

THE BRITISH EXPERIMENT

Those British imperialists, such as Joseph Chamberlain, who wanted Britain to be at the heart of an ever-closer Empire, also put forward monetary union as a way of achieving it. The Gold Standard worked as its exchange rate mechanism, but it was not until Chamberlain's sons' day, at the Ottawa Conference of 1932, that the Sterling Bloc was created. It was intended to defend Sterling's value in the post-Depression world economy by ensuring that all dominion and colonial reserves were held in pounds, with the exchange values of the various currencies pegged to sterling. (12) In the long run Britain did not benefit from her attempt to buck the world currency market, she merely held back colonial development and allowed outside pressures to build up which proved irresistible later on. It was this closed market that America was so desperate to destroy at Bretton Woods as the Second World War ended. The result of attempting to protect the currency, along with the tragic post-war fall in relative productivity, produced devaluations in 1949, 1967 and 1976. The unhappy experiences of the Sterling Bloc could teach the European Union much about the superiority of free currency competition over managed exchange rates, except that the greatest lesson we learn from history is that we don't learn history's lessons.

A SINISTER ATTEMPT

The Second World War saw another blueprint for a single European currency to be managed by a central bank. In 1942 the leading industrialists of the Third Reich, headed by Dr. Walter Funk, the President of the Reichsbank who was also the Reich Economics Minister, wrote a collection of essays on the future economic orientation of Europe after the Nazi victory. The book, entitled 'Europäische Wirtsgemeinschaft' ('European Economic Community'), contained proposals for common agricultural, trade, transport, industrial and monetary policies, as well as an all-powerful 'Europabank' (based, needless to say, on the Nazi "engine of state", the Reichsbank). In his chapter, Funk discussed 'The European Currency' and in a more detailed exposition by Dr Bernhard

Benning, the Director of Berlin's Reichs-Kredit-Gesellschaft, on 'European Currency Issues', the plans for 'Harmonisation of European Rates of Exchange' and then a 'European Currency Bloc' were spelt out. Fortunately this attempt to impose a single currency was also beaten off. (13)

CONCLUSION

History's experience of single currencies imposed by central authority tells us that they are powerful instruments. In national hands they can aid national liberation and even guarantee sovereign independence. Foisted on unwilling peoples for primarily political ends by supranational authorities, however, they can end in fostering precisely those nationalist impulses which they are intended to extinguish. In the case of today's heterogeneous, multilingual, economically-varied, racially diverse, recently-democratised, multi-sectarian, geographically vast continent, the experience of history suggests that a single currency for Europe would be an unmitigated disaster.

NOTES

1 Adam Smith, 'An Inquiry into the Nature and Causes of the Wealth of Nations' (1776), Book II, Chapter 2.

2 Paul Johnson in the 'Daily Mail', 11 February 1995.

3 Dictionary of National Biography (1901 version), Volume VI, p.469.

4 Anthony Padgen, 'Lords of All the World: Ideologies of Empire in Spain, Britain and France c1500-c1800' (1995), p.148.

5 Cambridge Modern History (1907), Volume IX, pp.27-8.

6 Barbara Tuchman, 'The First Salute' (1989), p.35.

7 Tuchman, ibid.

8 Smith, ibid.

9 Lawrence James, 'Rise and Fall of the British Empire' (1994), pp.340-1, 316-9.

10 David Thompson, 'Europe Since Napoleon' (1957), p.164.

11 Cambridge Modern History, Volume X, pp.294, 462.

12 James, ibid., p.456.

13 International Currency Review Occasional Paper, 4 September 1993.

Also available from Tecla:

John Redwood and Popular Conservatism (ISBN 0-948607-22-X).

This is a short book which provides a standard guide to John Redwood's ideas, aims, and policies. In order to make the book a handy work of reference, a brief career summary is included and an account of the events of June-July 1995 when he challenged John Major for the leadership of the Conservative Party. The complete text of the leadership campaign speeches is included, as well as a new interview, a discussion of his ideas, and commentaries on all his major books and articles.